The First Ten Pages

How to Adapt Your Novel Into a Screenplay

FRANK CATALANO

THE FIRST TEN PAGES
Copyright © 2009 / 2014 Frank Catalano
All rights reserved. No part of this book may be reproduced or transmitted in any form or by any means without written permission from the author.
ISBN-13: 9780692282892
ISBN-10: 0692282890
Lexington Avenue Press
www.lexingtonavepress.com
818-994-2779

BOOKS BY FRANK CATALANO

Art of the Monologue
Monologues they haven't heard yet

The Creative Audience
The collaborative role of the audience in the creation of the visual and performing arts

White Knight Black Night
Short monologues for auditions

The Resting Place
a play

Autumn Sweet
a play

Rand Unwrapped
Confessions of a Robotech Warrior

Che Che
A screenplay

Short Monologues for Auditions

THE FIRST TEN PAGES was first presented as part of the 25th Annual Writer's Conference sponsored by San Diego State University on February 6 through the 8th, 2009 at the Double Tree Hilton Hotel in Mission Hills, California. The following transcript was presented and recorded by Frank Catalano as part of the programs offered at the conference. This book is in part based upon this and other seminars presented by Mr. Catalano.

Writers of fiction and non-fiction and industry professionals from the publishing business primarily attended the 25th Annual Writer's Conference. Mr. Catalano's seminars focused upon those writers seeking to adapt their novels into screenplays. The complete list of seminar presentations by Frank Catalano for this conference is:

BOOK 1: WRITING GREAT CHARACTACTERS IN THE FIRST TEN PAGES
BOOK 2: WRITING ON YOUR FEET – IMPROVISATIONAL TECHNIQUES FOR WRITERs –Part 1
BOOK 3: START YOUR STORY AT THE END
BOOK 4: THE FIRST TEN PAGES
BOOK 5: BOOK TO SCREEN
BOOK 6: ACTING IT OUT – IMPROVISATIOINAL TECHNIQUES FOR WRITERS - Part 2
BOOK 7: WRITE GREAT DIALOGUE

TABLE OF CONTENTS

Section 1:	Introduction	1
Section 2:	Location Location Location	7
Section 3:	Creating Inevitability in the First Ten Pages	12
Section 4:	Let's Go to the Movies	19
Section 5:	Instant Gratification	29
Section 6:	Write Like You're a Pole Dancer in a Strip Club	37
Section 7:	The Road Not Taken	43
Section 8:	Your First Ten Pages Description, Action and Dialogue	47
Section 9:	A Rose by any other name Having the Right Title	55
Section 10:	Begin at the End	59

THE FIRST TEN PAGES

SAN DIEGO STATE UNIVERSITY
25th Annual Writers Conference

HOW TO ADAPT YOUR NOVEL INTO A SCREENPLAY

BOOK 4

Frank Catalano

Section 1

INTRODUCTION

Good afternoon, my name is Frank Catalano and this is The First Ten Pages... hopefully I'm in the right room. We me you never know. But even if I am in the wrong room, we will do this anyway.

(Audience laughter)

It's raining pretty hard out there today. I have one more seminar workshop this afternoon and then if the weather lets up, I will head back to Los Angeles today. Are you guys all okay? Is it a little warm for you in here?

Okay great. We're good to go. What I'm going to do first is tell you a little bit about myself and as I do this – we will multi task.

What I'm going to do get your email addresses so that I can send to you via email the materials we will be discussing today. Also, if you have any questions after you leave today's workshop... perhaps when you get home, you can email me and I will be happy to answer you. So, if you indicate your name and the email address that you would like to be contacted at, I will send you materials from our workshop today and upon receiving it, you will then have my email address.

First, let me introduce myself properly to you. My name is Frank Catalano. I am a college professor teaching at the School of Theatre (now School of Dramatic Arts as of 2012). I teach acting, writing and theatre and all different kinds of elements of presentational performance. I also teach Humanities courses that include visual and performing arts: painting, sculpture, film, television and audience studies. My acting classes are both on camera and stage. As a theatre producer/playwright I have had productions at the Beverly Hills Playhouse in Los Angeles and have had shows produced in New York City and other parts of the country.

In addition to academia, I was an executive at Warner Brothers Studios and Lorimar Productions probably the longest. I had various positions including consultancies, packaging, marketing and writing. I had what is called a **first look writing agreement** at Warner Brothers for the development of motion pictures and television productions. Working at a movie studio is a great experience. The studio provides a framework to develop everything you write although they are not obligated to produce it. So you set up shop there, you write, you work with other writers sometimes. But, the hard part of that process is that not very much gets actually made. In a large studio universe, producing was something totally different than writing. I just primarily focused on the writing.

I am also an author. *I have two books out: ART OF THE MONOLOGUE (2007). It's a theatre book for actors with original monologues and a large section on monologue performance theory. I've also had plays produced and published. I have a new play being published right now and I have a brand new book coming out this month called THE CREATIVE AUDIENCE – THE COLLABORATIVE ROLE OF THE AUDIENC IN THE CREATION OF THE VISUAL AND PERFORMING ARTS (2009) and so it is not being sold in the lobby.

*Since this 2009 presentation, Frank Catalano has published the following books:

ART OF THE MONOLOGUE (2007)
THE CREATIVE AUDIENCE (2009)
WHITE KNIGHT BLACK NIGHT – SHORT MONOLOGUES FOR AUDITIONS (2010)
AUTUMN SWEET – A PLAY (2011)
THE RESTING PLACE – A PLAY (2011)
RAND UNWRAPPED – CONFESSIONS OF A ROBOTECH WARRIOR (2012)
CHE CHE – A SCREENPLAY (2013)
SHORT MONOLOGUES FOR AUDITIONS (2013)
MYTHS AND TANGOS (2014)

My new book (The Creative Audience) covers a subject I have really been thinking about and actually we are going to talk a bit about it today. That is the creative role of the audience in the making of visual and performing arts. It takes into consideration the both the visual and performing arts including painting and advertising. But it also covers film, television and the Internet. How things are created today on the macro level almost in reverse. When someone comes up with a creative idea, it's really kind of tested first to see if the audience will respond positively to it. They do the same through polling in politics. Today, political leaders determine policy often by polling. They develop policy and then frame it in a certain way for public consumption to obtain the result they want to get. It doesn't mean they lie. It just means that information is just packaged a certain way. And it's going on right now, when we watch the news. Depending on "how" the information is presented determines how we react to it in the end. It also can be considered in writing – especially in what you guys are doing.

How many of you are active screenwriters – what I mean is actively developing content for television, film or the internet separate and apart from writing fiction?

(Several audience members raise their hands)

So then the rest of you are primarily novelists who want to adapt their material into screenplay format. How many of you fit that category?

(More audience members raise their hands)

… and lastly, is there anyone here trying to convert a screenplay into a novel.

(No audience members fit that category)

Okay, I just had to ask. Primarily then, you are novelists wanting to adapt your work into the screenplay format.

What I would like to focus on today is the concept of creating a screenplay from a larger work of fiction. Now we have discussed during this conference various means of developing and presenting material for production including pitches, treatment and submitting your script for coverage. All of these activities require that you be present for meetings to actually do the presentation of your idea. If you submit via mail, on line or through representation (that is not local) it becomes a daunting process at best.

I am not sure how many of you live locally. Where are you a from? Is anyone here from Los Angeles? How many from LA?

(No hands go up)
No one. How about the San Diego area?

(Several hands go up)

A few... and where else?

(Audience member raises their hand)

Where are you from?

(Audience member: "Utah.")

Okay. Anyplace else?

(Audience member: "Arizona")

(Audience member: "North Carolina")

North Carolina! And you?

(Audience member: "New York."

Great. What part? Upstate? I'm from Long Island... do you detect a slight New York accent?

(Audience laughter)

But I've out of New York for a very long time.

SECTION 2

LOCATION LOCATION LOCATION

I'm going to say this. Screenwriting is a lot like real estate... "LOCATION – LOCATION – LOCATION. Location is everything. I live in Los Angeles and I went into the bank one day and while waiting on line I was talking to someone I knew about her screenplay. As we talked I noticed that there was a large amount to people listening to our conversation. Other people on line, the tellers and the management staff... in short everybody was interested in our conversation because it had to do with her selling her screenplay. When I saw this, I said in an elevated tone, how many of you people are in the process of writing or already a screenplay. After everyone laughed a bit a large group of those listening raised their hands. I thought to myself... my goodness... almost everyone has a screenplay!

(Audience laughter)

The reason why I'm telling you this story is to illustrate that almost EVERYONE in Los Angeles is either writing a screenplay, wants to write a screenplay or has a relative or roommate that has a screenplay.

(Audience laughter)

For those of you who do not live in Los Angeles this fervor for writing screenplays and the biz is more than likely not as intense.

Why am I asking where you live? Because I am trying to gage your availability to physically market your script in person. Bottom line is that everyone is either doing it or wants to do it and a lot of the communication between writer and producer is done face to face. So what about those of you who don't live in Los Angeles? How can you get your ideas heard and read?

(Audience member: "What about if you have an agent?")

When you say agent, do you mean literary agent for your fiction books?

(Audience member: "Yes.")

That's fine… but remember if your representation does not have a relationship with the person or producer they are trying to get to read your project, they too will be operating from a disadvantage. Also, location is a factor. If your agent is in North Carolina they will not have the same access that a local agency might have. So what you want to think about is how to get your idea or screenplay in front of someone who will give it the attention and consideration that it deserves.

So I thought that an interesting seminar might be about how to do that. Assuming you are not in the room with the reader because you are not in Los Angeles — what can you do to hook the reader and make them want to read the whole script? Now I keep referring to the "reader" as opposed to the term "producer." Why? In most cases, if you can get your script to be considered by a producer, that person will not be the person who actually reads your material. Submitted material is often "covered" by professional readers or production company staff assigned to that function. This person will read your script and then prepare a professional report about it. The term for this practice is called "coverage." When coverage is done on your script, it is essentially a report prepared by a reader that includes a 1-2 page synopsis of your story, character breakdown and an evaluation as to whether it merits further consideration. Sometimes the reader will also suggest above the line cast or director. The report, like Yelp, rates your work quantitatively by specific categories that may include: title, main characters, supporting characters, setting, plot, budget and commercial viability.

As a screenwriter you have several challenges.

1. Getting your script in front of someone to be read.
2. Getting the reader to like or be interested enough in giving your script their fullest attention rather than rejecting outright.
3. Getting positive coverage so that your script can move to the next level.

So how can you accomplish that? How can you get your script past the reader?

The answer is that you have to get them up front within the first ten pages. If you have them at that point, you will be more likely to keep them through the end of the work.

You more than likely won't have the opportunity to pitch your idea in person, so you have to do within the screenplay format. Have you ever had this happen to you? You get a response from a producer or agent that tells you that would like to see ten pages of your work?

They say something like: "Send over ten pages… and if we like it… we will call you."

(Audience members nod in agreement)

The hardest part for me has always been which ten pages to send? Do I select the rip-roaring climax of the story or a pivotal point in the plot or just send them the first ten? Now earlier this week, I did a seminar entitled START YOUR STORY AT THE END. I think a few of you were attended that seminar and the theory behind that statement START YOUR STORY AT THE END is based upon starting your work at the most pivotal moment in your screenplay. The most exciting moment that pulls in the reader or audience and has the greatest possibility that they will want to go further and read the entire work. So that answer to my question about which ten pages to send them is simple. Send them the first ten pages. But make those first ten pages create the desire for anyone reading them to want to go on to the end to find out what happens.

Now I'm saying this to all of you in this room. Those who live in Arizona… North Carolina… New York… Utah and even San Diego – if you don't have the opportunity to be there to be on your feet, in the moment pitching your story, then you have got to let your script do the work for you.

We live in an immediate gratification society… television and the Internet have done this to us. Our attention span is short. If we don't get what we are looking for right away, we do a mental check out. We may be going through the motions but we are not really connected. So we have got to make our connections soon and make them meaningful.

You don't have a lot of time to do this in. So I have set the arbitrary length of ten pages. That's your goal, to connect irrevocably in ten pages. Create an air of inevitability -- after that, they will be connected and you will have them for the entire journey.

SECTION 3

CREATING INEVITABILITY IN THE FIRST TEN PAGES

One thing that we can all share in common is that we are all at one time or another members of an audience. We all are exposed to media… the movies, television and the Internet. Now I will ask you this. Put your audience hat on. Now, here's the question.

What about the first ten minutes or a motion picture or a television production? You sit there in a darkened room and experience the film or television show. Now think about how you reacted.

It's either you thought, this is interesting I want to experience more or this is boring and I'm thinking about eating a cookie. If it's television, you might reach over for the remote and just change the channel. One of my pet peeves in the television industry is when the new crop of fall shows premieres. During the first few episodes of each show, the writers spend an inordinate time introducing characters and character relationships at the expense of plot. The net effect is that these early shows are relegated into tedious scenes of character development. This is probably why almost all of the new shows fail to gain an audience and are cancelled. I'd like the networks to spread out the seasons with longer runs of episodes so that each new show can develop their characters in an interesting way and by doing so build and audience.

Every season, there are usually one or two breakaway hits while the rest fade away. Ask yourself this, what about those hits attract us to them? What elements do we identify with? What elements do they have that makes us keep coming back and want to know more. If we can figure that out, we can include these elements in your screenplays. Please remember, if we didn't like the beginning we wouldn't be back again to make them a hit.

Same question for the movies… what elements are present in the first ten minutes of a feature film that pull us in? In my other seminars we talked about beginnings that pull you in and make you want to see more. For example, the opening of the motion picture JAWS (1975) with a classic opening that pulls you in. https://www.youtube.com/watch?v=yrEvK-tv5OI

It's nighttime on Amity Beach. Chrissy, a young girl runs along the beach toward the water followed by her inebriated male friend. As she gets closer to the water, she removes her clothing, he stumbles after her, and then falls head over heals into the sand. She jumps into the water and swims outward.

Then we see a close up of her head popping out of the water as she yells out "come in the water!"

The next time we see here is from the point of view of the shark – she swims peacefully in the water as the shark gets closer and closer – as it does the now famous music intensifies. Then we see Chrissy one last time smiling just before her legs get tugged and pulled below the water. Then she let's out a blood horrific scream as she is dragged across the water. Then there is one brief moment, where it looks like she might make it, she grabs onto a harbor buoy but is snapped away and disappears beneath the water. A moment later, all is quiet and serene on the beach and water. All this happens within the first three minutes of the movie. It pulls the audience in so that they have to see more to find out what it was that pulled Chrissy into the water and how it will all be resolved at the end.

Okay, that's the final film. Now, what did the screenplay JAWS by Peter Benchley and Carl Gottlieb -- Based on novel by Peter Benchley look like for the same scene?

1   OVER BLACK   1

    Sounds of the inner spaces rushing forward.

    Then a splinter of blue light in the center of the picture.
    It breaks wide, showing the top and bottom a silhouetted
    curtain of razor sharp teeth suggesting that we are inside
    of a tremendous gullet, looking out at the onrushing under-
    sea world at night. HEAR a symphony of underwater sounds:

landslide, metabolic sounds, the rare and secret noises that
certain undersea species share with each other.

CUT TO

2   EXT. LIGHTHOUSE - NIGHT   2

   Caught in its blinding flash, the light moves on, fingering
   the fog. A lone buoy dongs somewhere out at sea.

3   EXT. AMITY MAINSTREET - NIGHT   3

   The quaint little resort town is quiet in the middle of the
   night. A ground fog rounds a corner and begins spreading
   toward us. It fills over sidewalks and streets like some
   Biblical plague.

4   EXT. THE SOUTH SHORE OF LONG ISLAND - NIGHT   4

   It is a pleasant, moonlit, windless night in mid-June. We see
   a long straight stretch of white beach. Behind the low dunes
   are the dark shapes of large expensive houses. The fog that
   has reached Amity proper is seen only as a low-hanging cloud
   that is pushing in from the sea. HEAR a number of voices sing-
   ing. It sounds like an Eastern University's Alma Mater.

5   ANOTHER ANGLE – BEACH   5

   A bonfire is blazing. Gathered around it are about a dozen
   young men and women who are merrily trading fight songs from

their respective universities. Two young people break away from the circle, Chrissie almost pulling a drunk and disorderly Tom Cassidy behind her.

6   CLOSEUP - CASSIDY   6

makes a clumsy try at kissing Christina but she laughs and ducks away.

7   ANOTHER PART OF THE BEACH   7

The fire, now one hundred yards in the b.g., silhouettes Chrissie running up a steep dune. Once there, she pauses to look at the ocean that we can only hear. Cassidy plods up the dune behind her, grossly out of shape.

Chrissie runs down a few steps, leaving Tom Cassidy reeling on the summit. Chrissie's dress, bra and panties fly toward Tom, who can't make a fist to catch them. The dress drapes over one half of his head. Soggily aroused, Cassidy struggles to get his shoe off.

But Chrissie is already in full flight toward the shore. In she goes, a delicate splash, surfacing in a cold ocean that is unusually placid. Chrissie pulls with her arms, drawing herself into deeper water.

That's when we see it. A gentle bulge in the water, a ripple that passes her a dozen feet away. A wave of pressure lifts her up and eases her down again. Her face shows the beginning of fear. Maybe it's Tom. She smiles and looks around for him, then her eyes go to the beach where Tom -- too drunk to stand -- one pant leg off, is struggling with his other shoe. Chrissie turns and starts for shore.

8   CLOSE - CHRISSIE   8

Her expression freezes. The water-lump is racing for her. It bolts her upright, out of the water to her hips, then slams her hard, whipping her in an upward arc of eight feet before she is jerked down to her open mouth. Another jolt to her floating hair. One hand claws the air, fingers trying to breathe, then it, too, is sucked below in a final and terrible jerking motion. HOLD on the churning froth of a baby whirl-pool until we are sure it is over.

9   ANGLE - CASSIDY   9

in his undershorts, laughing, turning in slow stoned circles, a prisoner in his orange windbreaker that seems to have him in a full Nelson. He stumbles to his knees.

As we read this today, we do so with the knowledge of the story and characters. However remember, when this story was first presented the reader and the audience did not have the familiar knowledge of JAWS and were spellbound by its story and characters. Stephen Spielberg took the basic idea that was included in the screenplay and the elaborated upon it – gave it tension and a sense of irony. However, the bottom line, is this opening compels us (even today) to want to know more, want to see more and ultimately find out what happens in the end. Think about the opening first ten pages of your script as if it were a movie trailer – a compacted version of what is to come.

If you are wondering how to do this?

Think about starting your script as if it were a movie trailer.

SECTION 4

LET'S GO TO THE MOVIES

Okay, so why would I want to frontload my screenplay with all the important elements of my story in the first ten pages?

If I do that, what will there be left to tell?

And why would I want to make my wonderful screenplay into a movie trailer?

Good questions and the answer for them all is the same.

So that you hook the person reading your script and you make them want (have to) read the rest of through to the end.

Let me ask you this… what is the purpose of a movie trailer?

(Audience member: "To get you to go see the movie."

Right and if you think about it. They are asking you to see the movie not immediately but sometime in the near future. How do they do that?

They make you a promise through the two to three minutes they have your attention.

If you see this movie it will be

A nail-biting thriller

A horror film that will frighten you

A love story that will make you cry

And they go one step further

They take what is unknown (you haven't seen it) and connect it to what is known that you are familiar with. We are familiar with stars, directors or Sequels (a continuation of a storyline and characters we already know).

A love story starring Brad Pitt – you may not know the story but you know Brad Pitt

A movie from Woody Allen – you may not know the story but you are familiar with Woody Allen's work.

The Expendables 1, 2 or 3 – does it really matter what the story is? You are familiar with all of the stars in the film and you know it will be an action picture.

So a movie trailer is a market tool used to connect an audience to a particular film at some future time.

Trailers pull us in with specific sounds and music to set the mood. Hard cutting so that they show us bits and pieces here and there but never truly reveal the entire plot. In short trailers tease us… into wanting more. Wanting more…

Everybody wants more of what they like. This makes me think of one of the greatest showman that ever lived Florenz Ziegfeld – who is best known for his Ziegfeld Follies. Now remember, Ziegfeld produced at the turn of the century in America – this was a time when there was a great formality in the way people behaved and dressed. But Ziegfeld was a master at knowing what the people wanted. So he came up with an idea to feature a half naked muscle man named Eugen Sandow to pose in a G-string on the stage. He was as naked as you could get without getting arrested. Of course women of the day, flocked to see THE GREAT SANDOW and some of them were even allowed to come up on the stage and squeeze his muscles – after which they promptly fainted.

Ziegfeld knew how to pull an audience in and make them stay. He knew that no mater what he did, sex would sell to audiences at that time. So that's what he did.

Now back to our screenplays. In our first ten pages we want to do pretty much the same thing. Introduce some compelling aspects of your character and story – but never give it all away. Remember the GREAT SANDOW – just give them enough to hook them and want more. Once you have them there – they will stay until the end. Also, think about JAWS – we never see the shark. We knows something is down beneath the water but we really don't know what. If we want to find out, we have to stay with the story and characters.

You I can't help but think of the opening sequence of the feature film THE GODFATHER (1972) which opens with the haunting melody of the Nino Rota Theme and then is followed with the close up on Bonesera the undertaker asking for the Godfather's help and more specifically "justice." https://www.youtube.com/watch?v=OIBpHO1gZgQ

Here is the opening scene written by Mario Puzo and Francis Ford Coppola in script form.

INT DAY: DON'S OFFICE (SUMMER 1945)

The PARAMOUNT Logo is presented austerely over a black background. There is a moment's hesitation, and then the simple words in white lettering:

THE GODFATHER

While this remains, we hear: "I believe in America." Suddenly we are watching in CLOSE VIEW, AMERIGO BONASERA, a man of sixty, dressed in a black suit, on the verge of great emotion.

> BONASERA
>
> America has made my fortune.

As he speaks, THE VIEW imperceptibly begins to loosen.

> BONASERA
>
> I raised my daughter in the American fashion; I gave her freedom, but taught her never to dishonor her family. She found a boy friend, not an Italian. She went to the movies with him, stayed out late. Two months ago he took her for a drive, with another boy friend. They made her drink whiskey and then they tried to take advantage of her. She resisted; she kept her honor. So they beat her like an animal. When I went to the hospital her nose was broken, her jaw was shattered and held together by wire, and she could not even weep because of the pain.

He can barely speak; he is weeping now.

> BONASERA
>
> I went to the Police like a good American. These two boys were arrested and brought to trial. The judge sentenced them to three years in prison, and suspended the

sentence. Suspended sentence!
They went free that very day. I
stood in the courtroom like a fool,
and those bastards, they smiled at
me. Then I said to my wife, for
Justice, we must go to The Godfather.

By now, THE VIEW is full, and we see Don Corleone's office in his home.

The blinds are closed, and so the room is dark, and with patterned shadows. We are watching BONASERA over the shoulder of DON CORLEONE. TOM HAGEN sits near a small table, examining some paperwork, and SONNY CORLEONE stands impatiently by the window nearest his father, sipping from a glass of wine. We can HEAR music, and the laughter and voices of many people outside.

DON CORLEONE
Bonasera, we know each other for
years, but this is the first time
you come to me for help. I don't
remember the last time you invited
me to your house for coffee...even
though our wives are friends.

BONASERA
What do you want of me? I'll give
you anything you want, but do what
I ask!

DON CORLEONE
And what is that Bonasera?

BONASERA whispers into the DON's ear.

DON CORLEONE
No. You ask for too much.

BONASERA
I ask for Justice.

DON CORLEONE
The Court gave you justice.

BONASERA
An eye for an eye!

DON CORLEONE
But your daughter is still alive.

                    BONASERA
            Then make them suffer as she
            suffers. How much shall I pay you.

Both HAGEN and SONNY react.

> DON CORLEONE
> You never think to protect yourself
> with real friends. You think it's
> enough to be an American. All
> right, the Police protects you,
> there are Courts of Law, so you
> don't need a friend like me.
> But now you come to me and say Don
> Corleone, you must give me justice.
> And you don't ask in respect or
> friendship. And you don't think to
> call me Godfather; instead you come
> to my house on the day my daughter
> is to be married and you ask me to
> do murder...for money.
>
> BONASERA
> America has been good to me...
>
> DON CORLEONE
> Then take the justice from the
> judge, the bitter with the sweet,
> Bonasera. But if you come to me
> with your friendship, your loyalty,
> then your enemies become my enemies,
> and then, believe me, they would
> fear you...

Slowly, Bonasera bows his head and murmurs.

> BONASERA
> Be my friend.

> DON CORLEONE
> Good. From me you'll get Justice.
>
> BONASERA
> Godfather.
>
> DON CORLEONE
> Some day, and that day may never
> come, I would like to call upon you
> to do me a service in return.

Here in this one scene we are provided with a glimpse of what is to come. The scene is compelling because we are only seeing bits and pieces and want to know more – we have to know what is going to happen next.

SECTION 5

INSTANT GRATIFICATION

Television has changed us irrevocably and we have come to expect everything we experience to happen immediately. We are not interested as much any more in the process but are more focused upon the result. We have connected instant gratification to pleasure.

Just give it to me now. I don't want to wait. We we are not fulfilled we become stressed out, unhappy and tense. To make matters worse, we fuel our instant gratification with the help of the latest technological device. Our IPhone, Blackberry, Ipad and Cloud give us everything we need at a moment's notice. If it takes to long, we pass on it. Think of the prologue for the Shakespeare tragedy ROMEO AND JULIET. The prologue like a movie trailer, kind of sets the audience up for what is about to happen on the stage.

PROLOGUE

Two households, both alike in dignity,
In fair Verona, where we lay our scene,
From ancient grudge break to new mutiny,
Where civil blood makes civil hands unclean.
From forth the fatal loins of these two foes
A pair of star-cross'd lovers take their life;
Whose misadventured piteous overthrows
Do with their death bury their parents' strife.
The fearful passage of their death-mark'd love,
And the continuance of their parents' rage,
Which, but their children's end, nought could remove,
Is now the two hours' traffic of our stage;
The which if you with patient ears attend,
What here shall miss, our toil shall strive to mend.

Now take that prologue today and try to put it in front of a feature film and audiences will say the following:

1. Get to it!
2. Can you show it to me instead?
3. Is the rest of this play going to be like this with long speeches?

Audiences will say "Okay, great... I'm outta here!"

(Audience laughter)

They would leave the theatre because the would say, that the prologue pretty much tells them what is going to happen and now that they know that why should they stay to see it.

You see what I am saying is that the audience doesn't care much about the process and the use of language – they are more concerned with the result and the ending. So you have to provide them with a pivotal moment but you don't show them how it turns out.
That's what we see in JAWS or THE GODFATHER.

So what I want to explore with you this morning is how you can take your novel or screenplay and find that pivotal moment of no return within the first ten pages of your script. A pivotal moment that will make your reader not want to put the script down. If that is the case, it won't matter if you have a pitch session or not. They will want to read your work until the ending. They will have no choice but to do so.

We want to create that hook in the first ten pages so they can't put it down. Not everyone will care or want to know about your story.

Yesterday, we talked about a writer who pitched a story idea (his only story idea) about the Russians landing on the moon first.

Producer: What have you got?

Writer: The Russians

Producer: What about the Russians?

Writer: They landed on the moon first.

Producer: Okay.

Writer: …and nobody knows about it!

(Brief silence)

Producer: Who gives a shit… what else have you got?

(Audience laughter)

That was it. The pitch was over and the writer left the room broken hearted. But what we can learn from this is that not everyone is going to love what you write. But if you write a compelling first ten pages with interesting characters and plot – you stand a chance to find someone.

What key elements of character and story must you have then in these first ten pages?
You have to provide them with character as in the example of the GODFATHER.

How many of you have gone to a film and we are all an audience. In the first ten minutes you don't have a clue as what is going on in the movie? Think about how you felt during those ten minutes – and you may have thought about leaving the movie. But then you think that you have paid for it so you stick it out. Now

THE FIRST TEN PAGES   33

a reader, doesn't have that problem. If your script bores them, they just read it a lot faster or they skim and then write their report.

Sometimes even the trailers do not connect to our interests. We sit in the movie theatre and say to ourselves. "That one looks good." Then the next one comes one and we think "No way, Jose!"

(Audience laughter)

Or… I'll wait for HBO. That means I won't even download it on pay per view for $5.99… I'll wait for it to come out on something I already pay for.

(Audience laughter)

(Audience member raises their hand)

Yes?

(Audience member: " What do you think of the film opening for Inglorious Bastards (2009)? What do you think about the first ten minutes?"

http://vimeo.com/67348832

Yes, I think this particular opening is exactly what I am talking about. This opening on its face value is a very simple meeting between a Nazi officer and a farmer but under its surface is filled with tension and terror. It doesn't hit you right over the head but the tension builds continually until the SS officer kills them all. Well, all except one.

With out that tension and immediacy we are doomed to disconnect. Our mind will take us somewhere else as it wanders away. We think of food (that's what I do), what we will do later that day, things we have to do the next day -- all of it. From time to time we might reconnect to the characters and story but as time goes on even that becomes harder to do. We are all part of the instant gratification crowd. Just think about the last time your Internet connection was slow. As that small line moved across the computer screen indicating how much time was left, you felt like your brain was going to explode.

"I can't believe this! It's taking two minutes to download this file! Two minutes!" We become obsessed with the speed of it all and forget that we may be connecting to another machine on the other side of the world!

(Audience laughter)

…and although only a few of you sitting here today will admit that you go into one movie at a multiplex – get board, leave and go into another movie in the same theatre.

(Audience laughter)

We all do it. We as writers have to get to it sooner and make it more compelling than ever before. We do it for our audience and readers but we also do it for ourselves. This conference here today is not one for Dentists – we are not talking about teeth or dental hygiene… we are talking about writing. But here's the rub.

You don't need a degree like a dentist to call yourself a writer. Whether or not they are really a writer is not the point. The point is that they all call themselves a writer. Hollywood, is filled with bank tellers, former hairdressers and maybe even a few dentists that call themselves writers. They all have a screenplay or a book and a story that they want to tell. If they don't have that, they have an idea… and Hollywood is filled with people that want to tell their story. In all fairness to the producers and readers, there are a lot of people trying to peddle screenplays in Hollywood. So if they act a little standoffish, please understand that's why they feel this way. Think of this about 30,000 – 50,000 scripts are registered with the Writer's Guild of America (WGA) each year. Then there are new writers who don't bother to register their work with the WGA that brings the numbers closer to 100,000. Out of that number only a handful – maybe fifty are ever moved into development. Now wait, I don't want you all to get up and leave thinking if all that I am saying is true, then why bother.

However, with all of those numbers, I am telling you that you can enhance your chances to be one of those few screenplays that are put into development by making your work more inevitable. What does inevitable mean? Oxford dictionary defines it as "Certain to happen."

You can make your script inevitable by creating interest, connection and loyalty to your idea. I am talking about loyalty beyond reason. Have you ever heard someone say… "I just love that movie… I loved it so much I want to see it again!" When someone loves something that is loyalty beyond reason. How do they get to love? They have a connection to the idea that goes beyond the ordinary, which connects, to them in an intellectual, emotional, physical or spiritual way.

You're thinking to yourself right now: "I could do that… I could really do that. But how can I? I can't even get anyone to even look at my work. So, how could they ever be connected?"

How many of you have an agent that represents your writing?

(Several audience members raise their hands)

Out of those of you that have literary agents, how many have had a script sold through the auspices of this agent.

(No hands)

None? Okay, I'm not surprised because it is very difficult for an out of town representative to get material read because they are in the publishing side of the business not the entertainment side of the business.

Yesterday, in the workshop seminar we did there was a very nice woman who told me that an agent represented her and that she liked her agent very much. However, although she liked the person who was her agent, she was totally disappointed in them. They weren't get her books read or sold. So, for those of you who are sitting here today in despair because of what I am telling you, don't feel bad if you don't have an agent.

I'd rather have "no" agent than one who is not or cannot get me results. Why don't they get results? Maybe they are only effective in certain areas of specialization or maybe they only have contacts at some publishers or maybe they are not very good at what they do. In any case that's not a problem for you because you are going to develop and idea – a book – a screenplay that is inevitable.

The only thing you need to do is to get your work out there by any means that you can. The universe will take care of the rest. Don't worry about rejection. Every time you get a "no" it brings you closer to "yes."

SECTION 6

WRITE LIKE YOU'RE A POLE DANCER IN A STRIP CLUB

We are all an audience. We said that. But we are all also consumers. Every morning when we get out of bed until we set our heads down at night – we are barraged with a cacophony of images and messages. These messages ask us: to buy certain items, to do certain things or behave in a certain way. A lot of you sitting here today are saying to yourself "Not me… I am not swayed at all." However, what if I say to this to you?

"Winston tastes good…" You would say?

(Audience: "Like a cigarette should!")

You know how old that slogan is? Probably the 1950's and they stopped running it in the early 1970's. But yet we still know it today. Even if we don't smoke. Why? Because it was hammered into our consciousness remorselessly in print, radio and television ads. So we know the slogan by heart and could even say that there is certain inevitability in it. That's what we have to do with our writing. We have got to get it out there no matter what and make it inevitable that it will be produced. They will have no other choice.

(Audience laughter)

Doesn't this sort of sound like one of those motivational seminars. In a way it is, I want you to commit to creating an exciting, compelling and inevitable first ten pages to your work. Why? Because you can do it and because you **should** do it! So let's stop thinking of ourselves as just writers. Let's also think of ourselves as consumers. When we are exposed to those remorseless ads that somehow take root in our minds – what are we actually exposed to?

A promise. No matter what we hear or see or taste or smell or touch, a promise is made to us. Buy this and your teeth will be whiter, do this and you will be thinner or smarter or look younger. Isn't that true?

(Audience nods in agreement)

So what if we were to write that way in the first ten pages of our work? Let your title and the first ten pages of your work intrigue the reader with a promise and take them right up to the moment when you will deliver that promise – but then don't fulfill it. Now I'm going to be inappropriate – just for a moment. Write your first ten pages as if you were a pole dancer in a strip club.

(Audience laughter)

I bet none of you thought I would ever say anything like that.

(Audience laughter)

Now I want to say that I know absolutely nothing about stripping or pole dancing. Is anyone here today a pole dancer or stripper?

(Audience laughter)

Just checking... could be your day job... or night job.

(Audience laughter)

I wrote a segment one time for, I think it was NYPD Blue and the producer said to me "you obviously have never gone to a strip club." And that is still true today. But here goes... I'm going to use this as an example.

(Audience laughter)

If you were watching a stripper and they came up on the stage and took all their clothes off in ten seconds – then would be just dancing up their naked – it would get boring because there would be no tension or no sense of mystery. Just a naked body on a pole going up and down... am I right?

(Audience laughter)

But, if they got up there and danced and took one little piece of clothing off at a time and just teased you – to see what you could through the see through mesh... they would create tension and interest. Why because we all want to see what they would reveal next.

(Audience laughter)

Well writing in this case is like stripping. You give them what they need a little at a time to pull them in, no more... no less. You need to write like you're a pole dancer in a strip club.

(Audience laughter)

No, really. Your goal is to keep them interested and engaged. You take them all the way through to page ten and the BANG! You stop. They are caught off guard and don't know what to do. All they know is the want... they have to see the rest. GIVE IT TO ME! You will "give it to them" but they will have to read the rest of your manuscript to get there.

Once they make the commitment to stay then you have them where you want them. Your tools are description, dialogue and action and you want to use them a tautly as possible. No waste... every word you include counts toward your goal of keeping your reader engaged. Anything more should be cut. You don't want to cut the heart of your work – somewhere in the middle is the answer. I have an exercise you can try at home. Take ten lines of description from your book and boil it down to just two lines without losing the tension, impact or meaning. Try that on a couple of passages to see how it feels.

(Audience member: "Aren't you cutting everything out of it?"
No...
(Audience member: "For the sake of brevity?")
No you shouldn't lose any of the original impact of your writing. In fact it becomes, if anything, more compelling. These opening ten pages are where you draw them into your characters and story.
- Let the reader know your location and setting
- Introduce your main characters
- Set up your premise. Give them an inkling of what is to be... just a peek (like the stripper.
- Set the tone of the piece – just like you would with a piece of music and give them a hint of how it might end.

A good example is SAVING PRIVATE RYAN (1998). The film opens with a cemetery scene and the hard cuts immediately into the American landing on Omaha Beach. You really get the end of the story and major character in the first three minutes of the film. As he makes his way, with his family following, to a specific grave, he finds it and tears well in in his. A moment later, literally through his eyes, we are transported back in time to D Day and Omaha Beach. In about the fourth minute of the film, we are introduced to the main character of the film Captain Miller (Tom Hanks). The rest of the movie takes the audience on a journey to that one moment at the cemetery.

https://www.youtube.com/watch?v=0HUf68gFGEE

So we have two elements operating here.
1. We create a compelling beginning in the first ten pages of the script. We introduce our main characters and story and create a sense of inevitability wanting our reader and audience to want to see it through to the end
2. We create a promise. What is a promise? It is an agreement to provide something in the future. If we set up our story as a thriller, a war movie, a romance. We have then to deliver that promise through to our ending. If we fail to do that, we have a problem.

I bought a book many years ago called THE NEXT TEN THOUSAND YEARS. I bought it on a rainy day like this, thinking that I would curl up and get a glimpse of the future. Where ever I was at the time (think I was in a hotel and there wasn't a great selection of books, so I figured what the heck? I'd like to know about the next ten thousand years.

(Audience laughter)

So, now I'm reading the book and am about half way through it, I realized that the book and its writer were a little bit crazy. As I read each chapter of the book, the premise of the next ten thousand years seemed farther and farther away. When he got to the chapter when they were going to dismantle Jupiter, I had enough and threw the book across the room against the wall where it remained until I checked out.

(Audience laughter)

Why was I angry? I will tell you. Because the promise on the cover of the book and the title stated that it was going to show me what it would be like in the next ten thousand years. Once I got half way through the book I realized that the promise made to me was not going to be kept. So I felt ripped off. I bought this book and the promise was not kept. The title and illustrated cover of space ships in space promised to tell how it was going to be in the future and then did not. Also, my time was wasted.

What does this story have to do with us? When we write our novel and then our screenplay there is an implicit promise made to an audience or reader. It starts with our title and then it begins with our very first page. When you think of your book or screenplay I want you to think about what your promise is to your audience. I would rather you have this clearly in your mind than a log line. I hate when they ask you: "What's your log line?" I hate the idea of an artificially cute log line that is designed to give the reader an idea (in a line) of what your story is about. I'd rather you tell them your promise. If you read this, this is what I promise you. I like this better. We can do log lines all day and they mean nothing.

Producer: What's your log line?
Writer: Moby Dick…
Producer: Right.
Writer: In outer space.
Producer: Great!
(Audience laughter)

What does that mean? I'm not sure. Our stories and characters are not served by a log line. Give the producer or reader something they can understand rather than reducing your work to a label or slogan. Instead, read my screenplay or invest in me and I promise you this will be an adventure you will never forget for the rest of your life. Or invest in me as a writer. If you don't like this script I have ten more stories I can talk to you about. Become that person, the one who writes the nail biting thrillers, the adventures or romantic love stories. Think of the late Nora Ephron was best known for her romantic comedies and was nominated three times for the Academy Award for Best Writing for WHEN HARRY MET SALLY (1989), AND SLEEPLESS IN SEATTLE (1993) and JULIA JULIA (2009). You can develop a promise around yourself for certain types of stories and characters.

Make a promise to your audience and keep it. Which takes us back to our pole dancer in a strip club. What does a pole dancer promise us? This goes back to our first premise. They promise us that we will see and experience something in the future. They take us through the motions bit by bit until the end. Let's change the way things are done.

Section 7

THE ROAD NOT TAKEN

As I said, at the start of our seminar today, I have had the opportunity to spend time at many of the large motion picture studios in Hollywood. I spent the longest time at Warner Brothers and had a reverence for all of the great films that had been created there during the golden age of Hollywood. As a small Italian child living in New York, I had an uncle that was a film collector and he taught me everything about Hollywood and movies. My uncle Marty loved movies so much that he built a small theatre in his home. I am talking about a real movie theatre with a screen, velvet seats and a stage. As a young child he would let me sit in the theatre by myself and play great films with great stars. I would see the likes of Errol Flynn, Humphrey Bogart, Betty Davis and Gary Cooper over and over again. These films and the studios they were created in became something that I loved and respected. So when I arrived at the Warner lot, I was very excited about the tradition that studio had. I knew most of the films they had ever made and I believed that it was a magical place.

What I didn't know was that Warners and other majors like 20th Century Fox, Paramount, MGM and Universal were modeled after major manufacturing companies such as GM and Ford. The old-line studio chiefs ran the production in the studios in Hollywood and the New York offices ran the business of movie distribution and exhibition. I always looked at the movie business as an art but really it was also a business and Warner Brothers was no difference. Back in the golden age of Hollywood, the major studios released 52 films per year for audiences all around the world. This is something we as writers can never forget. That the way things are done at major studios is driven by business over art. It doesn't mean that studios will make anything for a buck. They want to make quality product but the drive for the bottom line will always win over the drive for the creative hallmark. The old system was what they called a contract system where everyone was hired and put on contract. Today, it is a freelance system, where writers, producers and actors (above the line) are brought in for a particular project or series of projects and often are profit participants in that endeavor.

So movie producers and by extension producers want quality product that an audience will want to spend money on and see. I think we need to rethink the way we approach them. Let's start a new way of doing things. Let's develop our projects less on the creative level and more on the business level. If your novel has sales, which are respectable, that means there are people willing to spend money to read your story and characters. Perhaps one way to describe our work then is from a marketing approach – detailing the target audience segment and profit viability. I know you probably all hate what I'm saying but let's start a new of doing things. Let's think like we are producers – so that we can answer those questions in a producer's mind that will come up when there is coverage done on your novel or script.

Some ideas tug and the heart while other have an intellectual appeal. Have both areas covered. When you get back home after this weekend. Look at your work again from a fresh point of view. Pretend you are a producer and evaluate your own work on its strengths and weaknesses for reaching a certain segment of the audience, it's budget and it's ability to connect emotionally with an audience. Is it a story that an audience will want to see or is it something that you think is off the mainstream? If you are lucky enough to get a meeting with a producer, let's change the way things are done. Connect with them as a producer would both with the emotion of your story and the intellect of your idea about how the story will fit a particular audience. Let's change the way things are done. If there are rules let's break them. I'm not suggesting that you walk into a meeting and flip the desk over and say buy my screenplay or book. But I am suggesting that you connect with a potential producer on a different level. Tell them why they can produce your work – because it is good – but also because it will be successful.

And who doesn't want to win and be successful?

Also, after you tell them what you tell them. Let them tell you what they can add. It's important for them to collaborate with you on the vision. This way they will feel ownership in it and want to see it made in the end. Let them feel comfortable with your idea as if it were their own. However, don't be a "good soldier." What I mean here is that you have to stay true to your vision even if it means being rejected. No matter what you are told, as Robert Frost aptly put it at the end of his poem "The Road Not Taken."

I shall be telling this with a sigh
Somewhere ages and ages hence:
Two roads diverged in a wood,
and I, I took the one less traveled by,
And that has made all the difference.

Be true to your journey and never sell yourself short.

Now let's get back to your script. You may be thinking, what does all of this have to do with my script and the first ten pages. Okay, let's discuss this. What does a script contain?

Let me ask it a different way, what elements are present when you write a script? Okay, Description, Action and Dialogue – let's look at these.

SECTION 8

YOUR FIRST TEN PAGES
DESCRIPTION, ACTION AND DIALOGUE

Description, Action and Dialogue

You may be writing for a reader, a producer or an audience and you have got to give. And I've we stated before, that's where the ten pages come in. you have to create a hook in the beginning and once they are on board, they you can roll out any way you need to roll out. How do you get to this with character? Three ways. **Description, Action and Dialogue.** Essentially on the screen that boils down to what they do what they say, how they look, and what other characters say about them and the physical world they exist within. Your main character may say wonderful things about themselves, but they could be telling a lie. You have to show the truth. Let's talk about **DESCRIPTION.**

So, how is the best way to describe your characters in those first ten pages where your character has their initial introduction to the story? Right? So, you have to introduce them in a compelling way. In your novel you could and can take all the time you need. Went to boarding school in France, studied law – add little anecdotes. You don't have that much time and space in a screenplay. You have to cut to the chase.

INTERIOR – LIBRARY – DAY

Professor Muldoon, a crusty but benign college professor, dressed in tweed and loafers, holds an old book tightly as he hobbles down a long oak stairway into the the living room of the old English manor.

You do it all in one to three lines not a page and a half. That's it, you have to create the same impact that you would generate in a page and half description you might have in your novel. And Anthony Hopkins acts it out.

(Audience laughter)

Let's talk about that. Shall we? In your novel you have every detail covered so that you know who the characters are in every detail. Now you've got a screenplay and its all got to be in there but at around 120 pages. So you cut, but you don't want to strip everything out of it. You must capture the essence of your full character description that's in your book. What I'm saying is that you must keep the soul of your book alive and you get that 50 or 100 word description and you boil it down to five or ten words and that's the challenge. But, don't be a good soldier that writes their screenplay in 100 pages but in doing so; the end product has no life in it. You must keep the soul of your book alive and so you struggle to make sure you get in those five or ten lines of description that you don't lose any calories. It has to have the same fullness. The next element is ACTION.

Action is how your character moves in the space – the universe you have created for them. You don't have to be like "He walked slowly put one foot after another." You don't have to do that. Instead focus on something interesting about how your character does something. Some sort of interesting action that they do like the way they tie their tie (James Bond) pet a cat (The Godfather) or walk on a sidewalk (Jack Nicholson in AS GOOD AS IT GETS). But you can create action as it happens "on the fly" as your character does it. Do you remember the old television series COLUMBO (1968)?

(Audience laughter)

I can't believe you guys remember that? Okay, well you would want to put a little bit about that character's actions in your set up. And Detective Columbo was interesting to us because we always enjoyed the way he seemed to physically fumble through each situation he was in. There was a "fumbling" almost inept quality about the character that made his adversaries not take him very seriously. They though "this guy is a total dork." But we loved to see Columbo fumble through and solve every crime despite how carefully it was planned. Sherlock Holmes is the flip side, the Victorian side. Holmes is very formal, scientific and he observes using his five sense everything intently. All his fastidious actions come into play, So action is important because it shows something about your character's way of existing physically in their universe that makes them interesting and worthy of our time. And we can go through all sorts of things to achieve that. It could be that your character in the first ten pages – their relationship with another characters shows....

(Off stage Voice)

Ten minutes? Are you sure?

(Audience laughter)

In the writing class we did yesterday, we were improvising about the "space between people." Just the space can change the way your characters react to things within their universe. You know those people in New York City on the subway? The subway car is packed – standing room only – and they are this far away from one another.)

(Catalano moves very close to a male audience member – almost touches)

(Audience laughter)

Don't worry, I won't touch you...

(Audience laughter)

Unless you want me to?

(Audience laughter.)

They are this far away and it's not a problem. Try that in Los Angeles. Try to move that close to someone and see what happens. I was on line the other day at a store (waiting to check out) and some guy (who was in a hurry) came up right behind me. He very close, I could feel him breathing on me and pressing up against my butt.

(Audience laughter)

No nothing like that… he was (I assume) trying to get the line to move faster. I turned to him and said pressing up against me is not going to make the checkout person or the line any faster. He just moved back… no comment. Now the definition of personal space in Los Angeles and now is different let's say than riding the subway in New York City during the rush hour. This guy pressing up against me in line was a violation of my personal space while it might not have even been noticeable in another situation. Definition of space in Ohio, Los Angeles is different than in New York City, Tokyo or Paris. You can create visual element for your character before they even say one word. This really goes to my example of Meryl Streep in DOUBT. That kind of visual introduction says something about your character and how they move – that might take you several pages to achieve in a novel.

I recently attended a screening of the film CHEF (2014) that (without giving anything away here) is about a chef. The opening sequence of the film (as music plays) is a series of visual shots our main character preparing food – doing the slicing, dicing – all the things a chef would do. But this action was not casual, he was preparing with a sense of purpose – so you knew right away, even before the first word of dialogue was spoken that the meal he was preparing was an important one. He wasn't just cooking breakfast for himself… it was more than that – much more. You'll have to see the film, because you're not getting anything else out of me on CHEF. Have any of you seen it?

(Audience laughter)

Really, we should stop right now and all go to the movies!

(Audience laughter)

But we can't can we? Can we? So you want to open with your characters up front and make them interesting and compelling within that first ten pages or ten minutes of screening. You want the reader/audience to want to know more about them and why they are doing what they are doing. So ACTION is very important tool for you to use to connect your characters to your audience. The other element that is important is of course DIALOGUE.

DIALOGUE is important because it is one the ways (probably one of the most important) a character communicates with an audience and other characters in your story. Dialogue is one of the primary ways your audience gets to know all the things they need to know to be connected to the story. Also, dialogue can reveal things about the character themselves; do they have a dialect, what do they say about themselves, what do they say about others, are they always telling the truth or do they lie? How do they speak? Do they speak in shortened phrases like?

(Catalano does Joe Pesci imitation from Good Fellas (1990)

"You said I was funny? Funny like I'm a clown, I amuse you? I make you laugh? I'm here to amuse you? What do you mean funny, funny how? How am I funny?"

(Audience laughter)

That's one way of doing it. Or does your character speak in long-winded speeches like let's say Sherlock Holmes. Figure out how what they say and how they say it fits in to what you are trying to accomplish.

You can ask my brother just one simple question and he will go off for an hour or more on it. So, really, I don't like asking him anything... you know.

(Audience laughter)

"Hey, Bro... "I call him "Bro" which is term of endearment. "How was your day?" Then he looks at me and smiles as if to say I'm so glad you asked. "Well, I got up this morning, brushed my teeth and then after that..." I think to myself... please just the highlights – do you have to tell me everything?

Is this your character? So, how they speak dialogue is just as important as exposition and content. When you finally finish the introduction of your main character, I am assuming that your main character is going to be there. Right? So your character walks in and I don't know we were doing THE SOPRANOS yesterday. I kind of dressed for it today. Your character walks in on page two and speaks for the first time with a Jersey dialect: "How ya'doin?"

(Catalano moves)

And he moves within the space leading with chin and is hunched over a bit (like he's going to whisper something important in your ear) or your main character could be an attorney with a physically that is more upright (morally driven)

(Catalano moves again this time more upright and driven.)

"How are you today?"

No chest, no chin. Little details like play strongly or should I say visually. You bring over the characteristics of your novel but with less stated. You keep your character's quality; you don't lose it with abbreviation. It's just as detailed but the detail has been compressed into Description, Action and Dialogue. Guess what? All of these elements are visual and auditory. You have moved from an intellectual medium (your novel) where everything is happens and is created in your head (your imagination) to a primarily visual medium based in external stimuli.

So, you wouldn't say your character enters leading with his chin and right foot. This type of physicality is too clinical. You might instead describe it using visual metaphors. Something like "Joey G walks in the room like a predator ready to strike with his eyes focused on the prize." The metaphor compresses it all into one short section and you can come up with a much better metaphor than I just made up on the spot.

(Audience laughter)

Then, the cinematographer, actors and directors can see it as you see it (from your words) and use their own creative input to interpret it. You might be thinking, what if they interpret my writing in a way that is different than my interpretation? Interpretation is never going to be exact. You aren't going to like this, but often the different interpretations make the impact of the work better. As we have said before, as long as the spirit of your original work is intact, you're okay. And that's what you want to set up in the first ten pages.

SECTION 9

A ROSE BY ANY OTHER NAME
HAVING THE RIGHT TITLE

There was a project I was trying to get made at Warner Brothers many years ago called ROCKET MAN. It was one of those crazy projects – no matter what I had in the script – everyone that heard the name wanted to see the script. It was bandied about for several years and there are even two different versions of it – one as a television series and another as a feature film. So, if was such a great title, why didn't it get put into production? Easy answer, at the same time, the Disney Company was making and released a film called ROCKETEER (1991), which had a lot of buzz around it but in the end was kind of a box office dud.

It's important to mention here that my ROCKET MAN in no way resembled the Disney ROCKETEER. However, what was at one moment a title that brought interest to a project, in the next the word "rocket" in the title because it sound like "Rocketeer" brought it instant rejection. As Shakespeare said in Romeo and Juliet – "A rose by any other name would smell just as sweet."

(Audience laughter)

So, your title is important to this whole getting your work read in the first ten pages. Remember, the title is the first then they see and hear. Your title should connect with your reader on one or more of four levels of connection:

Intellectual:
The title should say something, which triggers their imagination and gives them an intellectual response such as – 12 Angry Men (1957), Schindler's List (1993), The Hunt for Red October (1990), Inconvenient Truth (2006) or Gravity (2013)

Emotional:
This title should evoke emotional response in the reader Jaws (1975), Meet the Parents (2000), Life is Beautiful (1997), The Notebook (2004) or the Hangover (2009, 2011, 2013).

Physical:
This title should evoke a sense of immediacy and change in the reader. Want to make them physically react to what they read and perhaps do something different in their life afterward: The Tingler (1959), War of the Worlds (1953, 2005), Jaws (1975), Night of the Living Dead (1968), JFK (1991) or Inconvenient Truth (2006).

Spiritual
This title should evoke a sense of questions in the readers mind about life and the world that they live in such as Gandhi (1982), Field of Dreams (1982) or Life of Pi (2012).

Titles can be long or short but should be clear in their connection to the reader. They should create in the reader a sense of anticipation that will drive them to open the script and begin to read it. A great title should pull them in and make them want to take the journey. Lastly, take a look at the current tile of your work and ask yourself the following questions:

1. Promise: Does your title make a promise to the reader of something that is to come? Does it fulfill a need, tell a story or explore a character? The Exorcist (1973), Gladiator (2000) or Blue Jasmine (2013).
2. Meaning: Is your title a literal description - The Day the Earth Stood Still- 1951 or is a metaphor for something else - Snow Falling Cedars – 1999? Maybe it's a combination like Shakespeare in Love (1999)?
3. Audience: Does your title speak to a specific audience? Cinderella (1950) focused upon children or Cinderella Man (2005) focused upon adults. Ask yourself what is the target audience for this idea and make sure your title speaks directly to that group. Thinking in terms of a "general audience" will get you nowhere.
4. Inevitable: Is your title inevitable? Make your title as something they must read and can't put down – Gone with the Wind (1939), King Kong (1933, 2005), Jaws (1975) and any of the Godfather films (1972, 1974 and 1990). These are titles they have to read or be left out of the loop.
5. Simplicity: The shorter the better. Use terms that get their attention and call upon them to act. Make the title put them right in the middle of it all – with no other choice – Jaws (1975), Jurassic Park (1993) or Inception (2010).

So your title is very important because it is the gateway in which a reader or audience will enter your story. I have a lot of friends that are writers that will wake up in the middle of the night and write down what they think at that moment is a great title. They have files in Microsoft Word with just lists of titles. Titles they may never use or may rely upon at some future date when they are writing something.

(Audience laughter)

I'm not kidding. Title is very important and should be thought of your first ten pages. So we all should start keeping a list of titles that you can use when you are developing a new story. Sometimes the story may come first and then the title will go on top or at other times you can start with the title and then the story will come out of it. You can also take words out of newspaper articles, storefronts, road signs or if you feel creative graffiti.

(Audience laughter)

I was stuck on the Hollywood freeway in bumper-to-bumper traffic about a month ago when there was this piece of graffiti spray painted in red over a tattered billboard. It read: "All you need is the Right Kind of Love." Now I know the Beatles probably said it shorter and better when they sang "All you need is Love." But I thought, what an odd message to find spray-painted on a billboard sign on the freeway. So, I wrote it down.

(Audience laughter)

I may never use it... but then again you never know. So I have it tucked away in a file, like one of those athletes sitting on the bench waiting to be called into the game.

(Audience member loud sneeze)

Bless you. So your title is extremely important.

SECTION 10

BEGIN AT THE END

Okay, we have come full circle here today with this topic of writing the first ten pages of your screenplay. Now I don't want you to go after this Annual Writer's Conference and rip apart your screenplay. I want you to think about just going back to the wall.

Do you guys know who Marcel Marceau was?

(Audience member: "He was some sort of pantomime artist.")

Right. He was a mime and referred to mime as the "art of silence," and he performed professionally worldwide for over 60 years. He had a term, which loosely meant going back to the wall. This was an exercise where the mime would be placed in an imaginary box. In order to create the illusion that would have to create what was one of the most elementary mime illusions – a wall. From that point on, once the illusion was achieved the mime could move on to create a room, another person, or a larger situation. Marceau believe that no matter how advanced he had become at his art, he always went back to the wall.

What he was saying was that he went back to the most rudimentary technique in order to create his illusions. What does this have to do with your script or book.

I want you to go back to the wall. Go back to the original idea that you had before you wrote a single word. Once you have established this point, I want you to create a simple linear plot and character outline. It can be chapter-to-chapter, character driven tracking entrances and exits of your character or scene list from a screenplay.

You can do this on cards, pieces of paper or on your laptop. The important thing is that you go back to the very beginning of your story and break it down all the way to the end. Ask your self these questions:

1. What is the true ending of your story? Point of no return?
2. What is the most exciting event in your storyline?
3. What is the point in your story that your characters reach a point of no return?

If you can find these specific places in your breakdown you can begin. If you can't find them, go back to the original idea again, and rework it until these points can be clearly identified. Now here's the tricky part. Take these three points in your story and identify one point within the three that all three intersect. That is, what point in your screenplay is the true ending, most exciting and point of no return? Once you find this point, there is where your screenplay should begin.

1. Does the title of your screenplay reflect this point of no return? It should– it is your promise.
2. Set up the kind of story and characters you are sharing with the reader. Is this a comedy, a drama or horror story.
3. Let the reader know your major character. Introduce them in an interesting way. Maybe they are hanging from a cliff or falling out of an airplane.
4. Set up your story and major conflict. Give your reader an opportunity to invest in the story by raising the stakes. Maybe your main character has only 24 hours to live.
5. Lastly, do you have a message to your story and characters – Love will conquer all? Or is this just entertainment – set it up during the first ten pages.

You might be thinking, if you start your story at the very end, then there will be nothing left to tell or show the audience. I am not saying starting your story at the very end. I am saying start it at the moment just before the end. Start them at that pivotal moment where there is no point of return and your characters must go forward or perish. That's where you start, then once they are on board, you can tell and show them all the details as you go along and then give the final ending at the very last moment.

Let's go back to your promise. Start them at the most pivotal moment in your story so you create their interest. They will want to know how it all turns out. That's your job... you have to tell and show them how it will turn out. That's your promise to them. It's a promise that must be kept.

So, now let's get to work!

I want to thank you all for being such a great group. I hope you enjoy the rest of the 25th Annual Writer's Conference.

(Audience Applause)

I think we have to leave this space but I will be in the hotel lobby if any of you have questions or comments.

Thank you again.

(Audience applause)

www.ingramcontent.com/pod-product-compliance
Lightning Source LLC
Chambersburg PA
CBHW060705030426
42337CB00017B/2772